THE
HAMMER
OF
WITCHES

Dagger Editions, an imprint of Caitlin Press Inc.
8100 Alderwood Road,
Halfmoon Bay, BC V0N 1Y1
www.daggereditions.com
www.caitlin-press.com

Text design by Sarah Corsie
Cover design by Vici Johnstone
Printed in Canada

Caitlin Press Inc. acknowledges financial support from the Government of Canada and the Canada Council for the Arts, and the Province of British Columbia through the British Columbia Arts Council and the Book Publisher's Tax Credit.

Library and Archives Canada Cataloguing in Publication

The hammer of witches : poems / by Kelly Rose Pflug-Back.
Pflug-Back, Kelly Rose, author.
Canadiana 20200224026 | ISBN 9781773860299 (softcover)

LCC PS8631.F58 H36 2020 | DDC C811/.6—dc23

THE HAMMER OF WITCHES

poems by
Kelly Rose Pflug-Back

Dagger Editions

Table of Contents

For Scarlett; *du bist mein traum in stiller nacht*

Malleus Maleficarum

We were witches once, you and I

stealing through the dark
on cat's paws
to taste the drink
of bitter mushrooms
on each others' lips.

They found our beds empty one night
and resolved to make us
their delicate quarry
tearing through the bracken til they found us
torch light stinging
our saucer-wide eyes.

It was morning when they killed us
and our hacked-off fingers
burrowed like pale grubs
into the earth below the gallows
as the villagers all shrieked and fled

our black skirts swinging above them
like cathedral bells.

No brave man would come to cut us down
and in our shadows, mushrooms grew

grey stalks like withered fingers
pushing through
the blood-dark dirt.

Your love is a heathen rite, I told you once
in a note I wrote
on a restaurant napkin
and never showed to you.

Bride of nothing
bride of wind
and pouring rain

god is in the long bones of your thighs
the spined shadows
your eyelashes cast
against your cheeks
when you sleep

the two of us lost together
still

in this forest
of tall buildings.

Miscarriage

In the hospital, I dreamed that death lay beside me

my face a pale cameo
in the wreath
of her powder-gloved hands.

Leech-wife, reaper
she bathed my hair in strange attars
in tinctures of dark, bitter roots

as the doctors reached inside me
to do their strange tampering
unravelling skeins of dyed wool,
tangled strands of bloody pearls
bound in yellowed twine

those mangled pieces of you and I
and never will be.

In every city where your mother ever lived, it was raining:
it was raining on the broad leaves of poplar trees
on the street where you grew up
and on the eaves of the building
where your grandfather died.

All winter I remember
how we warred beneath this roof—
my sadness filled whole rooms

nesting in the lint of empty cupboards
curled on its haunches
in the damp of the kitchen sink.

Perhaps when I am gone you will find a space in your life
shaped like this, I thought
a chalk outline of my heavy body.

The phone will ring and ring
and no one will answer

and you will find yourself wishing you never raised your voice
or slept all those nights

with your back turned to me

I am sorry, sir
but no one lives here by that name.

Our bodies are flowing columns of script, my love

pogroms, floods
world wars
have conspired to bring us here

into the lisp and stutter of this life's strange passage
into the respite of each other

and this
we must never forget.

After you and I have found ten thousand ways to hurt and mend each other

after dawn has paled over the world's mad wreckage
and my heart's landfill
flutters with the grey wings of gulls

after Autumn's tissue paper ghosts have blown free from bare fingerbone trees
and the department store Santas have closed their cotton wool eyes

after the trembling in my hands
at last, subsides

the party guests will grow tired of dancing
the patriarchs will ease themselves from creaking chairs
and button the buttons of their dark coats

and you and I will find ourselves
alone, laughing at nothing
in the third-floor rooms of your parents' house

where I will tell you that I love you, still
the way I did when we were children

I love you, still
the way I did when we were old.

For Dave

The day after you died
my son asked me to draw a picture of you
holding a blue balloon.

He said "give it to Dave, a blue balloon"
and drew a giant circle
connected
by a line
to your hand.

I imagined it pulling you up
through a cosmos
of scribbly crayon stars
and on
to that next big perhaps.

He's seen dead fish
and birds
a roadkill porcupine one time

but I don't think he really gets it
he seems to think you're somewhere waiting
just out of sight
on your way to come bring us soup, maybe
like you did a few weeks ago

when there was freezing rain outside
and we were stuck in the apartment alone
all week
with the flu.

You know, I don't really get it either
I keep thinking to myself, Dave *died*
that must be hard for him

I should text him and see
if there's anything he needs.

The last time we talked
you asked me
if I'd been writing at all

and I'd laughed and said, who has time for that

I don't
I never have time
for anything these days.

And now here I am wishing
I could have found an afternoon somehow

to take that trip across town

and show up at your door

with a big blue balloon
while you were still alive.

Phantasmagoria

She was beautiful to me, you know
but not the way she was to you.

We lived together
among those concrete tombstones

and when there were no forests left
we turned ourselves into landscapes

my eyelids closing, slow
as her fingertips brushed them
in dust of translucent green.

Butterflies dry their wings
on the bark
of winter trees
in city parks:

this depilated earth where I lost her.

You don't know it now,
but the desert is creeping up
on us all.

Don't feel bad for me, I laughed
when I caught you by your wrist
and kept you from leaving

I was never anybody's daughter

I strip off my clothes
and the stars, they just envelop me.

I strip off my clothes
and the men just throw their money down.

I take little pieces of them all, you know
credit card numbers,
the crescent moons of fingernail parings

their souls growing cold
in my nitrile-gloved hands.

Tonight is the longest night of the year
and my shadow casts a darker black
stretching long on the snow behind me.

You dream of my body in iridescent mesh
beaded with small constellations:

the magician's assistant
my high heels click like hooves
against the surface of the stage
and you feel nothing
when my long knife divides you

when I slide the black boxes
that hold your severed limbs
apart

& the sound of applause, somewhere
in shadowed alcoves
makes my painted lips curl.

I think everything is packaged meat to some people
blood they didn't have to spill, just paid for.

Yet still you want to play the hunter
the hairs on the back of your neck standing up
when you catch sight of my thin silhouette
on the road ahead of you.

But the wind lifts my hair
and nothing is as you expected;

like columns of smoke
I grow tall enough
to spare the moon from watching

a mirror of the cosmos
sprayed in red across new snow.

For T.

I remember the day,
alone in the bathrooms
you lifted the uniform's hem above your breasts
and showed me the roses tattooed on your chest

dark whorls unfurling around puckered scars
of entry wounds
where bullets sang through flesh, once
and sank themselves in bone
stopped shot by some blind fate from silencing, forever
the heart's sharp tongue.

In the solvent light of operating theatres
of interrogation rooms
you wept behind the mask
of a stranger's face

corrective excisions
invasive procedures
the grand striptease that comes
at the end of it all.

When snow's greyed lip pulls back from city sidewalks
I will return from this place
shuffling like a sleepwalker in the sallow warmth of winter sun

while the bark and rattle of automatic guns
still echoes in the dark
behind your eyelids
every time the cell doors slam.

Freedom, my tenuous concession
I would give it all away
to see you turn to smoke in their hands

a gust of torn paper eaten to lace by flames
carried high above the razor wire's clawed coils

houses, castles, roads, stone walls
all swept away
in the wake of your passing

and swallowed back
into that endless, healing night.

Tarantelle

Every day she pulls my body from the ground
and wrings the water from my clothes anew,
cradling my head in her hands
when she takes me to the river and lowers me in.
I am born again, she tells me
its surface troubled, broken
where she wades.

She wants me to forget my name
and press my cheek into her belly's smooth altar.
She wants to wrap the bones of fish into my winding sheet
and sow me in the ground like a seed,
my skull crowning from the dirt once the frost has thawed.

In her kitchen she smooths my hair
with a fishbone comb; I close my eyes
as she paints crude animal shapes on my body
with her set of stinging brushes
blunt hooves leaving thumbprint bruises
as they bound across my abdomen
away from the candle flame's paraffin torch.

I sleep in her arms, and my shadow dances
under a canopy of powerline transmission towers,
frost-hard earth
cracking the soles of my feet like old leather.

Small leaves will grow where the callous rends
and seeps my blood;
it rains in fat teardrops
from the fanned tips of my fingers,
beading like sweat on my skin
where the flames curl and lick.

She wants to cover me, she says
in pollen and spit
dead leaves and the carapaces of insects

spilling from
my open mouth:

her touch, first the fire
that razes cities
to the ground

then shade of the forest
that grows in its ruins.

Vanishing Act

In the dark that gathers beneath tattered awnings
the dead laugh amongst themselves
and pantomime my rigid walk

shuffling behind me
until I enter the pools of light
cast by street lamps
and they shy away.

When we first met
you said you were immortal;

the bones in your hands aligned
with distant constellations

you were born
beneath an auspicious sign.

You draped your neck in cheap gold
and pulled your sleeves down over your wrists
when I touched the flower-petal bruises
that ran along your veins

your past a tragic heroine
lying motionless
on the mattress between us

her ash-white lips
scabbed with flies.

Summer came, and plastic carnations littered the street
outside the tenement where we lived
every month another funeral

felled by bullets, or by sorrow's slow gnawing
felled in snowy forests
of opiate sleep.

My feet have graced worse places, I told you
slouching houses
where the heads of slain, beautiful deer
hung, glass-eyed on the walls
and I fled from my body every time the scratchy fabric
was pulled over my face.

World of simulacra
world of tired machines

imbibed with spirits, I grow calm
and soft around the edges

dust falling from my hair
as I separate its strands.

In a witch's mouth
any word can become a hex:

the church where you prostrate yourself
before nothing

the calm waters that swallow you up
while you burn

I am those.

After you fall asleep
I lie inside this circle drawn in chalk
and the animals that live
behind the cracked plaster walls
come press their wire-brush fur against me
in the dark.

Backlit by black candles
my outlines blur
and fade away:

I set off running, once
and have kept on running ever since

past farm land and pulp mills
past neon signs
still promising eternity

as easy as I leave you, now
in the last place
you will ever be.

Imposters

In real life I am just bones, Jennifer
wrapped in a shredded tarp beneath four feet of earth
in a culvert ditch somewhere in southern Ontario
dreaming that I met you.

In real life, I never ducked in time
or made it to the door fast enough
to slam it on his hand.

You and I never got to meet
or sit together in your kitchen
spooning powdered milk into our coffee
as we laugh.

Maybe you died too
the night he grabbed your ponytail
pulling you towards his car
in that parking lot in Scarborough.

You only dreamed you got away
and the sound of your children playing
in the next room
is a dream as well.

On some days I feel animated
so close to real
that I have everyone around me
fooled as well.

Then I see the reminders, like I always do:
my own face strange in the mirror;
my lover recoiling
when I brush his shoulder
with my cold hand.

Every day, I pass people like us
on the street, on the subway
and find myself wanting
to touch them through the fabric
of their winter coats

and say, It's alright.
I'm not here either.
You and I, we haven't been here
for a long, long time.

River

When you left
it rained for weeks in the town where I live
the bodies of fish writhing, everywhere on the pavement.

I held them in my hands as they gasped and drowned
houses, treetops, the sun behind its milky cataract
inverted in the serene black domes of their eyes.

We slept below the surface like sunken islands, in my dreams
and the shadows of oars dipped over our bodies

urchin spines fanning from the soft places behind my ears

your hair a moonless forest
alive with the movements of crenellated fins.

My ancestors were sea serpents, I told you once
and guided your hands to the frilled crests of bone
that still ridge my skull at the temples

coiled turrets of chain link fence,
the lichened beetle shells of cars

rising all around us
in the columned light.

Past the scrapyard behind my house
the river bloats with oil-sheened suds

shallows thick with frog spawn
mosquito larvae flinching
in the dark concavity of upended tractor tires.

On its rust-stained banks I watch the silhouettes of cranes and excavators
arch their brontosaurus necks

red sun sinking below the skyline's jagged teeth

as I walk alone along those striated lines
of fallen leaves, of broken plastic
left behind
by the receding tide.

My Bones' Cracked Abacus

1.
night spawns the shapes of dark birds
suspended legless on their wing tips,

loping like stilt walkers
ragged in their gait.

I saw the moon curve its ridged spine against your cheekbone once;
a crescent of bristled fork tines, spokes,
tendons forming ridges under the skin of my hands.
I thought of you while she combed my damp hair over my face,
a curtain of blond tatters to veil my eyes.

the birds walked hunched under their winter cloaks,
only graceful in flight.

they pull themselves, dripping
from the cluttered dark of your pupils,
leaving sparse-haired brush strokes
where their wet feathers drag.

2.
when I stood still they used to flock to my twisted arms.
my body was a filter, a valved artery for the world's slowing traffic.

they grinned under their beaked masks when I sang,
when my ribs creaked and opened.

a harp strung between broken teeth,
the striated palette.

3.
I hummed under your bow once,
an instrument gutted.

inside me is a world of oil-dark pistons,
a rhythm madder than the heart.
my hands unfold embossed in red seams,
anemone flowers petalled in boneless fingers.
this is where they cut me, I told you.
this is where the flesh-tone doll's parts were grafted;
blank ugly sutures
a torturer's braille.

4.
my body is scarred in botched attempts,
a city untouched by grace.

sometimes when I lie awake at night
I can still hear their scraping laughter.
her back arches,
the sky filled with battering wings.

I live on the banks of a tar-black river;
its silence swallows everything.

5.
she bunches the skirt around her hips,
crumpled gathers of white netting.
the birds take form under her hands,
bright-eyed in the pooling ink.
they tug like kites
until she cuts them from their puppet strings,
dusk flooded
with the clatter of hollow quills.

my flesh rasps, I tell her.
there is nothing that could appease me.

Birch

When you left I found a book on the shelf
full of drawings of birds.
I cut them out with my scissors
thinking I would make you a halo
if I could teach them to circle your forehead.
I closed my eyelids with masking tape
and walked with my arms stretched out
into the wind-snapped firs
and the white trunks of birches,
convinced that I could find you if you thought I wasn't looking,
still sitting cross-legged somewhere
catching moths with the flame of your lighter.

Holes in the Backdrop

I should bring you the different fevers of things,
paintboxes and wrapped bars of them—
slight variations of heart, sized appropriately and canned.
They dress in many colours;
his feet make the dead leaves noisy.
And a greyscale rain would wash away the small wars,
the spots where I emptied my pockets onto the sidewalk.
Bringing up messes of wet jewels or the eyes of birds maybe,
clinging by strands of newspaper to the cuffs of my shirt.
All these sad accessories, the rags are obvious.
Sometimes tin cans have perfectly formed and functional digestive systems.
I opened one once with a sharp thing
and disturbed the preservation of its beating, pulsing things.
All week, you could tell just by my complexion.
I'd sleep facing the closet door and
the white shirts liked to pretend to be ghosts,
flying up and removing him from my line of vision.
Already I could hear the birds battering themselves at his rib cage.
Once he coughed them out while sleeping, just on accident,
and little angels blinked on, in every corner of the room.
There were no more deaths in the family to pacify him
back to dreams of pharmacy keys and the contents of my pockets, after that,
so he shot a moon and stars worth of holes.
Immeasurable milligrams of ghost.
His dance partner was a dying flashlight, for the time being,
her cheeks like blown light bulbs,
a malfunctioning TV set lodged under each of her eyelids.
He woke up alone and dug the dirt from under his nails
with a little broken piece of her.
He must have thought that it was something else;
a thing for drawing with, maybe.

After the Fall

Outside these walls, a world still waits
where day and night revolve on their hidden axes
the pain and joy of our brittle lives
mapped out
in the lazy arabesques
of falling maple keys

in the wind-turned pirouettes of sneakers
strung up by their laces from the power lines
where the stooped shoulders
of old tenements
blot out the sun.

•

Mayflies bursting, glass-winged
from their husks

green consumed
in the fiery mantles
of autumn trees

I no longer believe
in any dialectics
besides these

moments of peace
like lulls in the assembly line

when I live through the memory
of your skin against mine

shadow-paintings of wild horses
running from the lights of passing cars
on the soot-blacked walls
of suburban underpasses

every vast and ancient magic
that this world of men has killed
and pined for

alive somewhere
just out of sight.

.

Beneath canopies of razor wire

the skinbirds plait each other's bleach-scalded hair
knotting the stems of daisies;

springtime for Hitler
and Germany

dark insignias
tattooed in pen ink
on their hands.

The leaves of stunted oaks yellow
and trace descending arcs into the mud

rain filling the indents worn by listless feet
on a dirt track that leads nowhere.

Each month I swell with distant tides
the body's rituals, strange and animal
in cloistered rooms
of antiseptic white.

At the nurse's wire-meshed window
I show the pills on my tongue
the empty cavity of my mouth
once I have swallowed

gloved fingers searching
between cheek and molar

every secret that I keep, smuggled
precious contraband
beneath my tongue.

Passing days haemorrhage
into one another

my eyelids prised open every morning
in the light of artificial dawn
while you, far from me
are the earth's darkened hemisphere
teeming cities of neon
washing over the sleeping planes
of your face.

Outside the realm of clumsy words
there are no such thing as endings
only new things made from the old.

I held the plastic phone
on my side of the plexiglass
and laughed,

what if we kissed
at the end of the world

or maybe just
in the church
in the town where I grew up

with all those stained glass windows
showing the bloody deaths
of saints

a light more beautiful
than all the heavens'
jealous rays.

Stone

Something has left you;
your most indefinable piece.

It has braced itself at your parted lips
and pulled itself free while you slept

waltzing, deaf
through the lightless world
of closed-off subway tunnels.

It pales a woman's last breath, like smoke
pushed forever
from her chest's closed bellows.

It flies in gusts
from the unknowable dark
of chimney pipes, of overturned top hats,
to coast on sooty coat-tail wings
passing sometimes
while you sleep

so close that it grazes the hairs on your chest
and wakes you
seconds too late.

There is violence
in the slow wilt of these stems;

in the warp and seethe of the skyline
and in the ragged gait of wire-thin animals
that meet your eyes in the city at night.

Your reason dances
on the head of a pin,
squirming on the tip
of sleep's hollow needle.

It curls itself in the small of your back
drawn through the dark
by your body's warmth.

Forget time's currents
and the channels they have wrought;
the twisted faces of these carousel horses
and the slow lull of their rocking.

Every night you lift sorrow's knees
around your waist,
drawing your own long shadow
into the daylight
where its motions
no longer mirror your own.

One day,
our human skins will grow too tired and worn
to be convincing anymore

and people will look at us like they did
before we ever learned to pretend.

Just tatter-cloaked shadows
hidden among the crows
that gather every day on the tiered pagoda roofs
of phone booths

and wait for the Chinatown market to close,
necks jerking at avocado rinds
and crusts of bread

trying to break the spine of the small animal
that instinct still tells them they hold.

A Chorus of Severed Pipes

When I was a kid, I threw a stone into the moon's reflection
and saw it break into a thousand sharp pieces.

It was dark, and the world sang to itself
to keep from being frightened.
Wheat stalks sighed under the thresher's blades,
a chorus of severed pipes.
The crickets and frogs kept time with one another;
I wrapped my arms around nothing
and waltzed circles through the corn rows
adrift in the harvest's beaconless sea.

I kept all the pieces I found
in a sack in the barn
where the pigeons battered, frantic in my chest.

Sunrise flicked its laughing tongue
through the interstices between gap-toothed rafters
and I knew that I could never make it whole again;

all those tarnish-bright shards
carried away in the silt of stream beds
winking at nothing
from the thatch of magpies' nests.

That's why there are still dark patches on the moon.
That's why the animals still call out to each other in the dark,

bullfrogs' throats stretched fat like pearls
while the crickets rub their thighs and sing.

Hepatomancy

Dawn lets fall the night's last fading shawls
& her body weeps
with cut-glass jewels

thighs a blush of rose
behind the white-blond of ostrich plumes.

In the city I part my hair down the center
like one of Ted Bundy's victims
& write you letters in my head:

your beauty is the flight paths of migrating geese
whose silhouettes flap, transient
against my closed eyelids.

I cried enough to flood the Euphrates
remembering the soft curves of your body

Tigris, Neander
black channels wending
the root systems of briers
down my painted cheeks.

Cosmetic,
like all things are cosmetic

eyelids swollen fat with bruise

hinged black legs of spiders fish-hooked
at the corners of my mouth.

In my poverty I clung to these illusions
forgetting words and the placement of objects;
names of whole cities.

My burning palms
my shirtwaist fire

I would have sold everything
to keep him.

Car stereos, cheap gold
engraved with strangers' names

divided portions of my flesh
wrapped up
in waxed brown paper
bound with packing twine.

In shop windows, bodies hang
exhumed of the red, bunched fruit of organs

like the halved carapaces
of spent missile shells
like grottoes to some bloody saint

jewelled with the iridescent wings
of flies.

Every morning
the streets fill with people
and I dream
of pressing my lips
to the burst hyacinth
of your mouth.

Spring would thaw the ground
and we both would fill with life again
pulsing
with the movement
of insects.

In my mind
I am monstrous

lurching with my arms outstretched
through the brittle celluloid
of film reels

staples glittering at the seams
of my skull

a mess of scar
too ugly to fake.

I am sewn together
from the flesh of many
and we ache.

Trash Goes in the Ground

I saw a woman who looked like you, the other day. Not the way you look now but the way you used to look back when I knew you, her long dust-brown hair blowing across her face. She was sitting on the stoop outside of the Mission, lighting one of those skinny hand-rolled cigarettes. The flame illuminating her face for a second, before the shadows swarmed her again. I took a snapshot of her in my mind, Michelle, because I hardly ever see you anymore. And when I do it's just from a distance, and you look so different now that I have to look away.

When I sleep I dream about searchlights drifting over the surface of the mill pond, touching the little ripples on the water and making it sparkle like cut glass. I dream about white teeth in a twisted-up red mouth, birds flying in a V across the darkening sky. If you were here maybe I could ask you what it all means. But you're not, Michelle, so I just press the heels of my hands into my eyes and wait for the images to leave me, like everything does in the end.

It was morning when they found his body, floating there. His spit-polished boots arranged all neatly on the platform at the top of the grain silo, like that was what he left instead of a note.

At first I thought about doing it too. I would crawl into the culvert pipe in the ravine with the silt and the old leaf skeletons underneath me, and I would just cry and cry. Touching the bottle of pills in my pocket, unscrewing the cap and then putting it back on. Everybody does it like that, because the pills are so easy to get. They just give them to anybody who asks, anybody who says they toss and turn at night or feel like they don't have a reason anymore.

I remember sitting with him on those broken chunks of concrete by the docks, outside the pools of light from the hydrogen lamps that stay on all night so people won't sleep there. I would take the 40oz from his hand every time he passed it to me and I would tell myself this was my sacrifice to him, something I would do so he didn't have to do it alone. Not everybody's pain can be dealt with gently, and I would remind myself that when I saw new cut marks on his inner arms, fresh gashes of red overlapping with years of older scars. We would just drink and drink and when we ran out of booze one time we went to the store and he stole some Listo, and we drank that too. It made me sick and delirious, the lights from the moon and the stars and the grain refinery all bleeding together, running like tears down to the horizon until my eyelids closed and blacked the world out for another night.

Here's the way it goes, he told me once: we used to leave behind legacies, but now all we leave behind is trash. Every plastic toothbrush, every ziplock bag and pop bottle. The lid of every cup of coffee we ever bought. It all just collects inside the earth, and it stays there, never going back into the rot like things are supposed to. Just filling up the distended tumours of landfills, the dust-choked fistulas of old subway tunnels and closed-off mines. Filling up the concrete halls of those underground rabbit warrens where they stick us all eventually, and if we're lucky one day we get let out again, at least for a while.

I look out at the landscape now, and everything is dumb with pain. It hangs like a fog, muffling the outlines of houses, of treetops and power lines. Muffling the black wings of wind turbines that churn and churn in the endless dark.

The night you told me what happened, Michelle, I said to myself that I would kill any man who ever wanted to make you his trash. I would kill any man who ever tried to put you in the ground like that.

When I can't sleep sometimes I go walking in the ravine, and I lie down underneath the gnarled old jack pine, in that hollow where some animal must have dug the dirt out. I just close my eyes and imagine its roots wrapping around me, sedating me with their pressure. Maybe he was wrong about everything being done for, because it's spring again now and I see clover and dandelions and little saplings growing everywhere. In the ditches and down by the wharf and even in the old reclamation sites. Flowers blooming in that contaminated dirt, that place men used until they said it was wrecked and abandoned it.

If you would just talk to me again, I would take you back. Even the way you are now, with all those pieces missing. I would pick wild roses for you from the highway embankments and I would stick the petals to your face with the wetness of your tears until you couldn't help yourself and laughed, even just a little bit. I would find a car somehow and we would just drive and drive, until we found that place from my dreams where the roads stop sprawling. I would brush your dust-brown hair out of your face with my fingertips and say, look. There's tiny shoots of green pushing up through the cracks. You don't have to believe me, Michelle, but I think that we're at the end of a cycle. And if you look hard enough, you can see it too. You can see the world starting to grow young again.

A Cure for the Water Trapped inside Your Body

I remember the weight
of those small, brittle bones
like broken eggshells in my hands—
something that can't withstand
even the force of being fit back together:

the window box flowers
collared in white eyelet cotton,
pleating to foetal buds again
when the sun starts to set

my stomach
a globe of tears.

We made graves
for each of your sorrows
in the folds of my abdomen, once

buried too close to the surface
so that in years of famine
the small mounds rose up,
embossed like braille
across my stomach.

Sometimes I traced the planes
of those hard, formless scars inside me
and wondered if I'd stayed with you too.

If the shame that spread
over everything I touched
still coats your body
like a milky thrush:

your hands braced forever
in the door frame;

every thrash and heave
of the dog-toothed sea
still rolling in the whites of my eyes.

Distance

He is no blunt instrument
no dulcimer

no pantheon or high arcana

no periodic table of alchemical signs.

He is not the house that I grew up in
or any one of the lost things
I cannot recover.

His face is not the calm repose
of some patrician death mask.
His hands are not plaster casts of themselves.

He could be the frantic incandescence
of lightning bugs
trapped inside Mason jars

river stones
schematic diagrams of stars

algorithms for machines
that imitate life.

He could be thousands of miles away by now
in Ganonoque or New York

his palms still burning when he thinks of me

a me less flawed in his memory

than the one who exists here, in Toronto
where time still passes
like it should.

1995

This is only time passing;
rain in the gutter and on the stiff bodies of dogs—
a thousand tiny hands against the windowpane.
I watch my chest cavity fill up with washed and ironed yellow suns
as you put out street lights and the bodies of fireflies with your
blunt fingertips,
wasted under the thousand shining points of Cassiopeia's exposed viscera.

We're being consumed without apology
by this dead field with its four churches,
its soft opera of torn paper caught in the back draft of gulls circling,
bringing sad news from home.

Pink-eyed mice gnaw at my bones
while the dust clots dance with trace amounts of your ghosts.
They plant themselves like spores
and sprout small white flowers, like the knuckle bones of dolls.
They grow even without light,
still thriving in the aftershock of your passing.

Makeshift Ballroom

People with eyes that big,
they're hardwired to love just about anyone
somebody's mother told me once,
pulling an expensive necklace from her tear duct.

I watched my feet for cracks in the pavement after that
but still I could feel that my back was changing shape.
I pricked my finger and fell asleep
thinking that I'd wake and mistake your pupils
for little safe houses at night
because of the windows reflected in them.
I breathed myself too high into somebody's thrashing green branches
and even that fatigued me;

casting something altogether removed,
perfect and antiseptic and trailing strings of little lights.

I think that you and I were never built for this dustless spill;
neither seraphim nor parasitic gulls

but atrophied tin soldiers
in this blue-choked parade of pretty girls.

Canadiana

My first ancestor came here

trailing ash
of burnt up bodies

all things between heaven and earth, redacted
inside the hide-bound covers
of his book.

The lord gave man
Dominion, it said

so he made a woman
from his rib
and called her
Wilderness

feet sinking
into riverbed's
black endometrium

as his robes
pooled around him

on the surface
of the water.

Sturgeon
walleye

we drove forever, you and I
past Chalk River
and Rabbit Blanket Lake

where grey moon stares down
at the car park

and the neon sign
on the church in the strip mall
still promises
eternity.

Crow spreads its wings
on the eaves
of another broken-down
rest stop

a voice on the radio muttering
something that sounds
like Purple Rain

as glow bugs hit the windshield
smearing
their incandescent guts.

Life is short
and long, all at once
like the drive from one end of Ontario
to the other

our secrets yawning
like abandoned cabins

bald patches of cut blocks
marring
the mountain's face.

My first ancestor
travelled north
for weeks

before he disappeared

all things baneful, beset by devils
in the endless, howling white
of an imagined landscape.

Among the tiered green skirts
of cedars
vine and bramble
reclaim the leaning skeleton
of a church .

its steeple furred
in lichens

reaching
for the sky.

Nothing lasts forever,
you told me once.
Nothing has yet,
and it's not about
to start now.

Sweet Mercy, Her Body an Ark of Wild Beasts

My life has been the tin ribbons
of a jaw harp,
its bent notes twanging
in the lightless space
cupped between my hands.

I've tried to make sense of it:
the button eyes of cloth animals,
frayed cotton straining
at their herniated stitches.

The bones of my face are a map
I told you
the plates of my skull
fused like petals at my crown

where the infantry closed their ranks
and anointed me in mortar dust.

I told you the truth:
before I knew you, I lived for years
as a sin eater.
Beauty was a charm
I would never inherit,
my palate's cracked seam
a cleft between floorboards
in the attic apartment
where we lived
before the war.

You never stared
at the palimpsest
of scrawled transgressions
that I was sure
still etched my body.

As a child, you told me
how you used to wake sometimes
to see a wax museum of saints
looming above your bed

the dark-haired Virgin standing over you,
her robes a swimming quilt
of fish and birds.

Their feathers are cursive, crested
in halved suns;

she pressed her palm
to your chest, once
and fear died inside you.

I wonder where the mark of her hand is now
watching hoarfrost bloom
against the panes
of a shattered city.

The world turns its black spokes,
and the wind
covers my tracks forever.

Daylilies wilt and bow their heads,
blight-palsied stalks
curling, clawed against my palm.

Maybe I am a corpse, like the others
they heap like sandbags
along the edges of their barricade.

Maybe I am an old man
who has blinded himself
painting portraits on eggshell fragments
with a single-hair brush

touching the clothes
you left folded in my room
until their texture
no longer recalls your body

and my hands, too
are cast into the insensate dark.

•

In my mind
I called you Lost.

I called you City of Ur

the bones of whales' ancestors
scattered through the floors
of now-parched Cretaceous seas.

The stelae of their backbones rise
like buzzard-ridden arbours,
spines whip-stitched
lacing between sun-bleached dunes.

I want the ululations of a thousand throats
to guide me across black waters
whose shores I'll never reach

a ghost of night overpasses
watching the headlights of transport trucks
pass through my body
before the dark under the train bridge
swallows them again.

I want to open my eyes
to see her staring down on me
from the grotto tattooed
on your sunken chest

frail and impossible, a hothouse flower
blooming in the nuclear heat.

I have bled, and seen a river
fork through this place.

I have watched lithograph smoke
spill from the barrels
of silenced guns
to curl in bows and lariats
around her heart-shaped face;

foetal buds pushing through cracked asphalt,
the bones of ploughshares rusting
in soil too anaemic
for even the grass
to anchor its roots in.

Somewhere, the sun rises on a world
no longer drawn
as if by some hand

enamoured
of human pain.

Morning in the Necropolis

When I came back
I was transparent

the root systems
of necrophagic plants
pulsing, blue
beneath my skin.

Pale membranes of flesh
had closed
over my eyes
as though I'd been gone
all that time
somewhere dark;

my fingers curling back
into my palms
at any sudden light or noise

like the eye-stalks
of invertebrates.

Every day I would run my hands
over my body
and discover another little piece of me, gone:

shorn locks of hair
toes severed at the last joint

my two silver molars
pried loose by travellers, kept as talismans
to ward off poverty or death.

I walked with a limp
when I came back, one foot
numb like I'd slept on it wrong
for the past hundred years.

I was thinner than I'd ever been

flesh caving in
around the juts
of my skull.

You look amazing, everyone said.
What's your secret?

•

Nothing was like I remembered
when I came back:
all the holes in the chain-link fence
wired shut

torn tarpaulins
fluttering on pallet frames
in a night
where no fires
are left burning.

Eyes of the fox flash, small moons
repelling the light
of passing cars

the shape of some small animal clutched, still
in its mouth:
we adapt
because we have to

prone among the hulking shadows
of glass towers
of earth-moving machines.

When you know how to wait
for long enough
things don't matter
the way they used to;

January below the underpass
or nuclear winter,
the tears I cried
because everyone I loved
was gone
when I came back.

When the next epoch dawns
I will grow a new set of teeth

long and jutting
from my laughing mouth

a shadow
that escapes your vision
when you turn your head.

Go ahead and tell
no one would believe you

that I'm risen, walking here again;
that I never really left.

Skrattasker

Seething, he pulls himself from sea-rock

spinal fluid
of the deer
spilling, moon-white
from his lips

a winter storm
and in its eye, the warmth
of one shadowed embrace:

bring life, again
to the frozen earth.

Trance, they say
is woman stuff
the warp and weft of things
the world's axis
in the turning
of the weaver's distaff.

Beneath the ground
where the heaviest creatures walk

darkness itself
will be his husband

pale radix of the oak forest
exposed nerves
of some flayed thing

the universe's ten thousand hands
each of them
holding
a gleaming white thread.

When night falls
he will emerge
walking swathed
in veils of mist:

desiccated mushroom;
a sensation
of flight.

Against roiling clouds
the blackbirds circle. Dissolution

as he lays with his face
in tangled hair
of dead grasses

knife cleaving
soft flesh
of inner thigh,
a blood marriage.

Lifetimes from now
the caustic tears
of melting glaciers
will pool in the giant's clavicle

shorelines choked
with the bodies
of dead fish.

Fire marks the first attempt
at his life

the king's soldiers
making the sign of the cross
when he rises
from the rafters
of the burning hall.

Captured a second time, he will not survive:
the serpent that encircles
the earth
grows restless already.

Immersed in frigid tides
his bound hands
twist against each other;

around him
the other men sleep
with their faces
below the water.

Let go, her voice whispers
and he does

the flames
of her hair
all around him

peace, at last reflected
in the hanged man's pale, inverted face.

In the entrails of the mountains
she surrounds him
smelling of hearth
and sheep's wool.

Receiver of the dead
she lifts the veil
from his face
and smiles

never one to refuse
a blood sacrifice.

What I Learned from You about Love

Among the frigid tinsel stars
of Christmastime
I picture you, in childhood

huddled in the dark that waits
somewhere past the northern lights

flannel blankets
stitched with all the words
we sent you
close around your face

and on the sky's great pastel screen
Bugs Bunny walks, laughing
from another pyrotechnic misadventure:

all the futures that could have been
and this is the one
that happened

that laughter every time
and then an end
I don't want to picture

and you, laughing still
as you departed
although none of us
could hear it.

Maybe in death's storm-wet forest
Pleistocene mammals
bow their vast, horned heads

surround you with the musk
of their rough fur
and sleep, content
in knowing.

Maybe you're there
with your family
and those paper masks
have all been lifted
off their faces

borne like lanterns
into midnight branches

their arms a wreath around you
a sorry you never got to hear.

I go there still,
to all those places you're not

footprints in the mud among the cowslips
where dew beads the yarrow stalks
that grow over old chemical dumps

and nothing
makes any sense.

I wonder sometimes
if you were just waiting
to step on that landmine
inside your own head

knowing there would come a time
when the burden
would reach
its terminal weight.

I have stood on the shoulder
of enough highways to know this:
if you close your eyes, you can hear it sometimes
a distant, deep rumble, a feeling

that something very big
is coming
vast as an ocean
or the first breath
of a newborn mouse
searching in its mother's fur
for milk

stars and planets
and space debris
dancing in the endless black
of its closed eyes.

Listen,

you told us not to be sad
and I'm not.

How lucky it is to be born
at the end of all artifice

to know, in this half-broken heart
that beats, for now

that this is all there is,
all there needs
to be.

The Book of Jonah

Awash in heavy rain
the sailors cut the throats
of porcine cargo
hoping to be spared.

Plunged into brackish black
I leave them
past baleen stalactites, esophageal
rumination

the belly's hot cavern where
I paw through memory

broken pieces of plastic
to which emotion was attached, once;
the tiny hand of a doll,
a sea of bright confetti
a hundred disinflated red balloons,
shot of elasticity.

The whale's ribs creak
as it labours to breathe

old enough
to remember a time
when it was not like this.

For three days and three nights
it carried me
before heaving itself onto
the shores of Nineveh;

I struggled
from its carcass
and walked ashore

rebuked
by god
and yet unscathed:

a siege is coming
and this time none of us
will be spared.

The Night with the Cows

Suspended
in the starry fluid
of its mother's womb

the unborn calf
knows nothing
of cramped feedlots
or the stench
of blood
that clings
in grated floors.

Dreaming migratory paths
worn by generations
of hooves

across grasslands
long since covered
by onramps
and Walmart parking lots

it shifts,
eyes darting
behind
black-lashed lids.

This world is not a good place
for cows;

it hasn't been
for a while now.

Some people
have said
that the universe
is a cow

that existence
itself
began
with a cow.

How could we forget
that their horns make the shape
of the crescent moon.

The Vedas
are texts
of cattle herders

and before gods walked the earth
the frost giants
of the Eddas
too
were nourished
by a cow.

Pregnant
with impossible futures
her belly swing
as she kicks
until the door
of the livestock trailer
bursts open

panicked hooves to the grass
in the new moon's dark
where she will lick afterbirth
from her new baby

born in a field
beneath electrical towers

the stars above them
as white
as milk.

Grimoire

We met again
in the season of goodbyes

in late August's mortuary garden
among
exposed masses
of root.

The body of a bat
embraces itself
cocooned in leather wings

weightless as a wasp's gall,
or the seed-head of a daisy

torn white cotton
of sow's thistle
clinging to my dress.

Love had to be like this, to you
the softness, the barb

caught in my skin
drawing beads
of red blood.

Flowers bloom
where my fingers
press

a map of
veined petals

burst
for me.

I have touched your bones,
felt their hard ridges
when I reached
into your ribcage

where your heart
beats some rhythm that lives
in the back part of your brain
clawed and bristling.

Mysterium tremendum

the metal spider
crawls across your skin

a crucible
where nothing
is profane.

Sun stains the dead leaves
golden
stitched
with alchemical signs

and morning, again
finds me
in your bed
in a nest
of shed, metallic scales

never beast enough
for you.

The Only Prayer

Among the cornfield's swaying rows
moon-eyed cats
leave blood
and scattered feathers

feral, filling the hay lofts
with their squalling young.

In the barn,
the thresher sleeps
with its knife-toothed grin;

it was 3am when you told me
in a voice
that was almost not there
everything
that happened.

I've seen bodies
left behind by poachers;
It was like that

nothing but the hide removed
everything else wasted
a bloody carcass
where insects land.

In church basements
yellowed women would regard me
from the corners of their eyes

serving scalloped potatoes
and canned fruit

the spiders
in the corners of the room
encasing gnats
in pills
of cool gauze.

A rainbow
is supposed to be god's promise

there will never be another flood
but here we are
with the sea levels rising

while men on TV
sell rapture insurance
a years' worth of provisions
sealed in plastic tubs
guaranteed to float.

I remember now, red sliver
of autumn moon
a faceless smile;

the scarecrows
casting cruciform shadows

and your father
doesn't know
where you are.

I wanted things to get easier for you
and they never did

the only boy I knew
who didn't pull the wings
off flies.

This was the only prayer
I ever spoke:

that in the forest
you might find
a gentle god;

submerge your face
below the water
and see what I saw

that the dirt can just lift
right off you

among the shapes
of twisted bicycle frames
rusted shopping carts

bags of trash, weighted down
by river stones

a sacredness, still
in this place
where everything
people have thrown
over the bridge
ends up.

Genus: Insectivora

Insects have long memories

coming back
to the same two-millimetre crack
in the plaster

for generations.

I turn on the lights
and they scatter:

insects,
the shadows of insects

the crawling music
of legs and paper wings,

the black soot
that they leave
in every corner.

Listen, I died here a long time ago
and I've just been haunting the place
ever since

sitting on the dryers
in the basement
staring at my phone.

That light you think you see sometimes
and then it's gone
when you look again,
that's all it is;

I felt death's bony hand
close around my thigh, once

and I just laughed, and said
at least someone wants me.

I'm one of those ghosts,
that's stuck
doing the same repetitive motion
forever

that's the only reason
I still talk to you at all.

For A.

Awash in neon light
this is the altar
where broken men come
to scatter the contents of their pockets

crisp bills like fallen leaves
printed with the faces of other grey and empty men
necktie-garroted and faithless

heavy with confessions
that slough from your shoulders like nothing
as you laugh

their palms sweating as they burn
knowing that to touch you, just once
would be the closest they will come
to knowing god.

Acknowledgements

The Hammer of Witches was completed with the help of funding from the Ontario Arts Council's Writers' Reserve program.

"My Bones' Cracked Abacus" was previously published in *The 2011 Rhysling Anthology: The Best Science Fiction, Fantasy, and Horror Poetry of 2010.*

About the Author

Jehad Miro photo

KELLY ROSE PFLUG-BACK's fiction, poetry, and essays have been published in a variety of publications and anthologies, such as *Counterpunch, Huffington Post, Fifth Estate* magazine, *This Magazine, Briarpatch, Imaginarium Speculative Fiction,* The Vancouver Media Co-op, *CrimethInc* and more, and her work has received awards and nominations from the Rhysling Foundation, the P.K. Page Irwin Foundation, and the Great Canadian Literary Hunt. Pflug-Back holds a Bachelor in Human Rights and Human Diversity from Wilfrid Laurier University and a Masters in Development Studies from York University, where she studied the relationship between resource extraction and colonialism. Her poetry chapbook, *These Burning Streets*, was published with Combustion Press in 2012. Pflug-Back lives in Toronto.